I0410470

Letters To My Father

By

M.J. Flemming

authorHOUSE™

1663 LIBERTY DRIVE, SUITE 200
BLOOMINGTON, INDIANA 47403
(800) 839-8640
WWW.AUTHORHOUSE.COM

This book is a work of non-fiction. Names of people and places have been changed to protect their privacy.

© 2004 M.J. Flemming
All Rights Reserved.

No part of this book may be reproduced, stored in a retrieval system, or transmitted by any means without the written permission of the author.

First published by AuthorHouse 10/12/04

ISBN: 1-4208-0122-8 (sc)

Printed in the United States of America
Bloomington, Indiana

This book is printed on acid-free paper.

ALL SCRIPTURE REFERENCES ARE TAKEN FROM THE NEW AMERICAN STANDARD VERSION OF THE BIBLE

TABLE OF CONTENTS

FORWARD

When God is calling us, whether it be for the first time or if He is calling us to Holiness and a closer walk with him we need to keep in mind that there are no "accidents" but that instead each step is orchestrated by God to bring us into a personal relationship with Him. So here you are, about to embark on an adventure different to any you have ever known. I am going to take you through bits and pieces of my life. Be prepared, because some of this is going to sound very familiar to you. You are going to cry some, but you will laugh too. You may get angry some, but that's okay because your gonna let some things go also. I will take you into my childhood where you will share my pain with me, but I will also take you into my present where you can join in my victory dance. This book is for you, keep this in mind. You will see that God has never left you, even in the lowest points of your life. You will see that God has wonderful plans for your future. You will see GOD in this book. He put this on my heart to write and put this in your hands to read. Its okay if you find some parts a little difficult to get through. You should try being on the other end and writing about it. I have opened up my heart to you. I have chosen to do away with pride and shame and instead I will bare my heart and soul to you in the hopes that you may come to a better understanding of the depth of Gods great love for………….you. Come now, into my yesterdays and lets hold hands through this and keep our eyes up towards Heaven, where we will find our healing, hope, faith, mercy and never ending love. Are you ready for this? Yes, you are……..now begins the LETTERS TO MY FATHER…….

LETTER #1.....

Dear Father,

Guess what Father? Today I was born. Although I can't actually hold a pen or paper, as a matter of fact I really can't even think for myself yet, I wanted to get this letter to you any way to let you know that I have arrived. OF course, you already know this, but even at the time of my birth, I have a special place within my heart for you and wanted to start corresponding right away.

I am born with long black hair and green eyes. I am born in a small mission hospital (about the size of a house) in Jos Nigeria, Africa. Mom and Dad are missionaries here and big brother and sister are already here waiting for me. I saw them looking at me through the crib bars. I heard big sister call me "Timmy," I guess it is because I have so much hair she thinks I am a boy. She is only three herself, so it's okay. Big brother is just smiling at me as he is sucking on his bottle gazing in on me. He is not yet two years old, so it's okay if he sucks the bottle still. Since we are in Africa, we drink goat milk in our bottles. There are lots of camels and snakes around. I am surrounded by beautiful kids and grownups, they have the most beautiful chocolate skin and they love me and fight over holding me.

Well, I just wanted to let you know that I made it, I am here, thanks to you. I am looking forward to my future to see what wonderful plans you have for me. I know that you love me and you will never let me out of your sight. Until later….

love,
your little girl

Dear daughter,

Yes. I know that you have arrived safely. You are a gift that I have given to your family and to my world, but there will come times when you will forget this. I love you, I have sacrificed all for your love, so that we can be together forever. You are right in assuming that I have great and wonderful plans for your future, but once again this too you will forget from time to time. Even in those times when you will turn from me and forget the plans that I have for you I will still love you and guide you, I will never leave you……..love,

Your pappa father

"For I know that plans that I have for you, declares the Lord, plans for welfare and not for calamity to give you a future and a hope." Jeremiah 29:11

LETTER #2.....

Dear Father,

Good morning Father. I am six months old now and you have just saved my life. We are back in the states now, I am sorry that I had to leave Africa, I will never know its full beauty now, unless I can return one day as an adult and visit my birthplace. We had to come back to the states though, because I was very sick. All three of us were very sick, Big sister, big brother and me. We all had malaria. I had it the worst as a matter of fact I heard mommy crying and talking to daddy about me dying. That's why we came back to the states, things looked pretty bad, I was totally dehydrated, weak and I wasn't expected to live, so I guess it was better for me to die in the states than over seas.

I was very sick on the big airplane. I was hanging in a little basket above mommy and I could hear her crying and talking to you. You heard her to, didn't you? You fixed everything. Big brother and sister were already starting to feel better on the plane and when the plane finally landed and my mommy took my basket down and looked in on me I was all better. A miracle for us.....a token of love from you.

Well, Father, I guess that you really do have wonderful plans for me and my future. You have just saved my life and I wanted to thank you for that. I love you, you are a wonderful Father.

love,
your little girl

Dear daughter,

You are so welcome. It was a pleasure restoring your health, but I don't ever want you to be scared if you should ever become really sick again. What my people call death I call coming home. One day you will close your eyes for the last time on earth, but when you open them I will be standing in front of you with open arms. You will never know death, only eternity. Before that day comes, you will grow up to become a Godly daughter and a true servant, the enemy does not like you already, but I have sent angels to watch over you and fight for you. Don't worry about tomorrow, just continue to be my little girl and enjoy life. I love you and I will always save you…I will never leave you.

Love
your pappa Father

"BE GRACIOUS TO ME, O GOD, BE GRACIOUS TO ME, FOR MY SOUL TAKES REFUGE IN THEE; AND IN THE SHADOW OF THY WINGS I WILL TAKE REFUGE, UNTIL DESTRUCTION PASSES BY"

PSALM 57:1

LETTER #3…..

Dear Father,

    I am four years old now. I am growing really fast. I am a good girl Father…..aren't I? I thought that I was a good girl, but something happened today and now I don't know anymore. I don't know how to tell you this, but I think that I did something bad today. I haven't told anyone about this Father….can you keep a secret? I am ashamed to tell you this…but I am also scared of it and I know that you are big and strong and that You can help me and you are the best secret keeper in the world. Well here it goes, I hope that you aren't mad at me when I get done telling you about this.

    My daddy is gone out of town again. He works in the city and last night my mommy went somewhere with a friend. She had one of her friends baby-sit us. Big brother is almost six now and big sister is seven, anyway I think they were in the living room watching T.V. and I was already in my room in bed. For whatever reason I was not asleep yet, I think that I could kind of feel something was wrong. Then this friend of mommy's and daddy's came into my room. He was a grown man and he walked over to my bed and looked at me. I smiled at him at first, Father, because I knew him and I thought that he was just checking on me, but then I started to feel uncomfortable. Oh Father, I feel so dirty, I don't know how to tell you this, you are so clean and good and this is so bad and dirty, but if I don't tell you I think that I will die inside and won't be able to ever smile or laugh again. Father, he (that bad man) touched me down there. He just stood there touching me where I go potty, I don't know how I know, but it was very wrong. I just stared up at him with my big four year old eyes, scared to speak or move. I didn't understand Father. I still don't. He didn't touch me for very long then he left my room and he didn't come back in. Please don't be mad at me Father. I didn't ask him or even want him to come in my room and I feel sick at the thought that he did. I'm not going to tell mommy or daddy or anybody else, but you. Can we please keep this a secret? I know that I am asking for a lot, but I need your help with one more thing…Please don't let that bad man into my house ever again… please. If I ever see him again I am going to run and hide and probably throw up. I am also confused, Father, Am I bad now too? I didn't want to do this bad thing and I am very mad at myself. I wish this thing never happened. Can you reverse time in my heart, so that my heart will not remember these feelings that are hurting me right now. Can you make my heart forget and My mind not remember? I could see myself lying there looking so small in my bed and I could feel how big my eyes were. I was a like a small animal that someone kicked or caged. Am I an animal Father? Why me? What about the bad man? I don't think he was supposed to do that. It just didn't feel right. And why am I scared that mommy and daddy won't like me anymore if I tell them? This is too hard of a thing for a four year old to figure out....so will you figure it all out for me Father? Thank you...I love you...do you still love me?

love,

your little girl

P.S. don't forget to keep the bad man away....please, please!

Dear daughter,

Oh honey, I do still love you. You are my little girl, my precious daughter through adoption. Of course I love you sweetie, and I want you to listen to me very closely and hear my words...Do not feel ashamed for what happened. This was a bad thing that this man did to you, but I did not let any of his bad spread to you. You are still pure and innocent, you are white as snow, radiant and beautiful. There is innocence in your laughter and goodness in your smile. I will not let the bad man take that away from you, nor will I let him take you away from me. I am watching you. There are many of my children who are lost and listen to the enemy and who want and do bad things. There are many bad men and what happened to you also happens to a lot of my little girls...but I am in control. I need you to help some of these other little girls when you grow up. You will have common ground with them. It was a bad thing, but you are not bad, you are a good little girl. Even though it was a bad thing, I can turn it around for the good. You are going to go through many bad things as you grow up, but I will save you each and every time and I will turn them around for the good. I need for you to remember one thing through all of these hard times….I love you and I will never leave you. Don't forget this honey, keep my words close in your heart…for they are your protection.

love,

your Pappa Father

P.S. Oh, and don't worry about the bad man….He will never walk into your house again. I am sending troops to keep him out.

"DELIVER ME FROM MY ENEMIES, O MY GOD, SET ME SECURELY ON HIGH, AWAY FROM THOSE WHO RISE UP AGAINST ME. DELIVER ME FROM THOSE WHO DO INIQUITY, AND SAVE ME FROM MEN OF BLOODSHED. FOR BEHOLD, THEY HAVE SET AN AMBUSH FOR MY LIFE: FIERCE MEN LAUNCH AN ATTACK AGAINST ME. NOT FOR MY TRANSGRESSION NOR FOR MY SIN O LORD, FOR NO GUILT OF MINE, THEY RUN AND SET THEMSELVES AGAINST ME, AROUSE THYSELF TO HELP ME AND SEE."

PSALMS 59:1-4

LETTER #4

Dear Father,

Hello Father. How are you today? I bet that you are really busy aren't you? Daddy said that you never sleep, boy that is busy. Well I am almost six now. There are good things and bad things that have been happening. First, the really good thing. I have a new baby sister. She is so pretty. We all love her very much. Mommy even lets me carry her if I am real careful. Something was wrong when she was born, she was too little and she had to stay in the hospital for a week. The day that we went and picked her up was a wonderful day. Now there are four of us kids. Big brother and big sister help take care of baby sister. They are eight and nine now. They have to help take care of her because daddy and mommy are too busy fighting. They yell a lot and they both drink and then yell some more. They make us cry when they fight, once they even started hitting each other. Father, I know that they are good people. They are the best daddy and mommy in the world and do you remember all of the good things that they did when they were in Africa telling everyone about you? Well, maybe if you do remember, you could help them. I haven't seen them kiss or hug in a long time. I feel bad for baby sister. I don't want her to cry or be unhappy. Can you help us because its really scary when grownups act like kids, because then who will

take care of us all? I think that you will help us. I am
sad and I cry, but I can feel a little smile in my heart. I
think its called faith….faith in you. You have already
saved me so many times from a bunch of crummy
stuff so I am getting used to you coming to the rescue.
I hope that you don't mind, but I am waiting for you
again.

Father, I really don't want you to be mad at daddy
or mommy. They are my daddy and mommy and I
love them and need them. I know that this is just a
bad time, but I can remember a lot of good times that
they have given me and my brother and sisters. They
have always loved on us and hugged us and they tell
us all the time how precious we are to them. They
always find food for us to eat and they tell us about
you all the time. They have never hurt us in anyway
and that is why we hurt now, because they are hurting.
So can you fix things once again? I don't want daddy
to go away and I don't want mommy to keep crying.
Thank you again, Pappa Father. I will never stop
needing you and I will never stop thanking you. Did
you know that you are my Hero?

love,
your little girl

Dear daughter,

I am with you. I am in your house and in your
hearts. I am also in your mommy and daddy's hearts.
I know that this is hard for you to understand, but
mommy and daddy are people just like you and they
make mistakes, but you are right in the observation

that they do indeed love the four of you dearly. Don't forget that. Don't be mad at them and continue to talk to me about them and I will stop this storm in your life and a new day will dawn for you soon, I am happy to hear that you have a smile in your heart even if there are tears in your eyes. Yes, that is faith and my peace (which is a calmness in hard times because you trust me). I am not mad at your mommy and daddy, as a matter of fact, I love them as much as I love You. One day you are going to see that I love my children unconditionally. I love you when you make mistakes, when you fight, when you cry and even when you hurt others. I will always love you and your precious family. I don't want you to worry about dad or mom. I will help them. As for you, don't trouble your tender little heart, Because even when things at home are out of control, I am not. I am big and I am always in control. I love you.

love,
your Pappa Father, your God.

"PEACE I LEAVE WITH YOU; MY PEACE I GIVE TO YOU; NOT AS THE WORLD GIVES, DO I GIVE TO YOU. LET NOT YOUR HEART BE TROUBLED, NOR LET IT BE FEARFUL."
JOHN 14:27

LETTER #5

Dear Father,

Oh boy Father, I have some big news for you today. We were in a bad flood yesterday. It was crazy, kind of scary, but I knew that you were still as big and strong as you have always been and you gave us a way out. By the way, I am still six years old, but I think that I have grown a lot since I first turned six. I have learned that I can find a laugh deep inside of me when I am crying. I have found some comforting force inside of me when I have been really scared and I have just been playing all the time with my brother and sisters. This is because I know that you are gonna help mommy and daddy work things out. So, you see, I have been doing a lot of growing up since the last time I wrote you.

Now, I want to tell you about the flood. It rained all of last week. Daddy is back in city working, so he doesn't even know about this yet. You are the first one that I have gotten to tell it to. Anyway, yesterday neighbors started coming by our house saying that they were getting worried because the river had begun to overflow onto the banks and that their yards were quickly filling up with water. As you know, we live in a bowl, at least that is what I call it. It is really a valley totally surrounded by big, big mountains that you have made, (and may I say Father, that I am very impressed with your craftsmanship). Anyway, just as it was getting dark, some of our neighbors came over, there was about fifteen of us in all. The grownups all decided that we should leave immediately and start walking up the mountain. There is a man that lives in a cabin up on the side of the mountain and that's where we decided to go. Mommy let us grab whatever we could carry. She was carrying baby sister. Big sister had a bundle of clothes and some snacks, big brother had his guinea pig in his jacket and I was carrying my dolls. We walked in the pouring rain and even though the waters were rising behind us, and it was very dark and we were cold, we were also a little excited. I even laughed and joked with big brother. There were a few minutes that I got scared, but here is the neat thing. I knew that you made this big mountain for us. That you knew that one day we would need a big mountain to climb so that we could head to safety. My heart was actually light. I felt so safe, the higher that we climbed, maybe because I know that your throne is in heaven and I was feeling a little closer to you each step that I took. I think that I have just felt that peace and faith that you had been telling me about. I trusted that big, strong mountain like I trust you. I have just realized that you have always been my big, strong mountain.

We made it to the cabin and spent the night there. Two other families and us. When we woke up today, the rain had stopped and the sun was out so we walked back down the big mountain. When we got to our house it was dry on the inside. Now I know that the water was rising last night, yet our house is dry. So I believe that I have you to thank for making an invisible dam around our house. You are so cool. I love you tons and I just wanted to tell you about the flood. Thank you Pappa, thank you Father. Once again, you have saved me and I love you in a very special way.

love,
your little girl

Dear daughter,

It makes me happy that you like my creations. I think that my big mountains are cool too.

Yes, I knew that you would need that mountain one day. You see, I always give my children a way out of every bad situation. Sometimes that way out comes fast, other times it takes a while for you to get out. Something that you will learn when you grow some more, is that I will never let more happen to you than you can handle. When things are getting tough that's when I gladly step in and finish getting you to safety.

One day all the mountains will be gone, but I will stand strong forever. There will be different kinds of flood waters that will surround you later, but I will pick you up then too, and put you on a high, safe place because I love you and I will never leave you.

love,
your Pappa Father, your Pappa God

P.S. your welcome for keeping your house dry. I am glad that you noticed my invisible dam.

"HE SENT FROM ON HIGH, HE TOOK ME;
HE DREW ME OUT OF MANY WATERS. HE
DELIVERED ME FROM MY STRONG ENEMY,
AND FROM THOSE WHO HATED ME, FOR
THEY WERE TOO MIGHTY FOR ME. THEY
CONFRONTED ME IN THE DAY OF MY
CALAMITY, BUT THE LORD WAS MY STAY. HE
BROUGHT ME FORTH ALSO INTO A BROAD
PLACE; HE RESCUED ME, BECAUSE HE
DELIGHTED IN ME."

PSALMS 18:16-19

LETTER #6…..

Dear Father,

I am calling out to you from a scary darkness. I am eight years old now and I am homeless. Dad and mom broke up and I don't know where dad is right now. We have moved several times during and since their breakup. Now we have run out of money and are homeless. I am scared Father.

In the past month I or rather we (big brother, big sister, little sister and mom) have slept on a mattress in the woods, in railroad cars and now we are in an abandoned house in the middle of a big city and we are cold and hungry. At first we stayed on the old mattress in the woods, but the mosquitoes were really bad and were eating us alive, their buzzing was so loud it was scary, like one of those sci fi movies. Big brother and I were tasting bark and grass while our stomachs were growling real loud. We could no longer stay there mom knew we needed help, so we walked into the city. Mom found some change and we went into a donut shop. Each of kids got one donut and we shared a glass of milk. Mom didn't eat anything, she said that she wasn't hungry and it's a good thing because I know that she didn't have a penny left. It was weird though, because her stomach was growling awful loud for her not being hungry.

We were tired from walking and we had a little something in our tummies, so we were sleepy. Mom looked around when we got outside in search of a place for us to rest. I remember people walking by us and either staring at us or looking the other way and pretending not to see us. I guess it was because our faces were dirty, our clothes had holes and stickers in them and I know that my hair looked like a birds nest. Anyway, Mom led us to the railroad tracks and we climbed up into a railroad car and cuddled up together and slept. When I awoke, we were moving. I guess mom wanted to leave the town we were in and get us as far away as she could from the mattress and those horrible mosquitoes.

When the train stopped it was night time. There was a man walking from car to car checking inside of them for people, when he got to the car that we were in he opened the door and shone his flashlight in and pointed it right at us. We were all shaking, scared of going to jail, the man stood there a minute then at the top of his lungs he yelled "all clear." He pretended not to see us, and I want to thank you for that nice man.

Now we are in an abandoned house. We got off of the train as soon as the man had left and we are now in a big city. We walked all night until morning, then we began to walk around looking for churches to help us. We found a couple, but for some reason or another, we walked away empty handed. Finally a church gave us a bag of food then we found an abandoned house and that is where I am now. It is night time and it is storming. Big brother has just gotten a can beans open with his little pocket knife.

Oh Father, these are the best beans that I have ever had, they are so good, thank you.

I know that I am always needing something from you, but that is only because you have already come to my rescue so many times and Father, right now you are the only constant, permanent hope in my life. So, here I am again….crying out to you. I don't want to stay in this house tonight. Please help us…please, please. I know that you will find us a better place to sleep, but if there isn't any place can you please make this place safe for the night. I am so scared Papa God, I am so sad, but you have told me that all things work out for the good to those who love you and that is the one thing I have to hold on to….my love for you.

Well, it's storming really bad right now and I am going to go over and sit with my brother and sisters and mom and wait for the morning to come. I will also be waiting to hear from you. Please help me to see what is going on, what is my life about, what is important, what does my future look like. I need you Father for I am very scared.

love,
your little girl

Dear daughter,

Do not be afraid of the darkness or the storms. These are my creations. I have created you to be a light in the darkness. Your family is there with you and they to are a light. Comfort one another. Don't let the storm scare you. My storms are really quite amazing. My lightening is beautiful and my rain waters the earth. If you look closely, you can see my greatness in the storm. I am great and if I can create such a marvelous act of nature, I can certainly take care of you, can't I?

There are many of my children who did not even have a can of beans tonight to eat. Pray for them and let me say I was very impressed when you thanked me for the beans that you did have. I will take care of you, my daughter and when you are older you will remember all of the times that I came to you rescue and you will love me even more. Until then, I don't want you to be afraid of being hungry or finding a place to sleep. Don't you remember that when my Son was born, he too had no place to be born in or to sleep in after he was born. He was born in a barn with animals on a cold night also, so are you among the best of company. Just hold on my little girl and watch what I am going to do with your life. I am with you now and I will be with you always….I will never leave you.

love,
your Papa God, your Father

"CONSIDER THE LILIES, HOW THEY GROW; THEY NEITHER TOIL NOR SPIN; BUT I TELL YOU, EVEN SOLOMON IN ALL HIS GLORY DID NOT CLOTHE HIMSELF LIKE ONE OF THESE. BUT IF GOD SO ARRAYS THE GRASS IN THE FIELD, WHICH IS ALIVE TODAY AND TOMORROW IS THROWN INTO THE FURNACE, HOW MUCH MORE WILL

HE CLOTHE YOU, O MEN OF LITTLE FAITH!
AND DO NOT SEEK WHAT YOU SHALL EAT,
AND WHAT YOU SHALL DRINK, AND DO NOT
KEEP WORRYING. FOR ALL THESE THINGS
THE NATIONS OF THE WORLD EAGERLY
SEEK; BUT YOUR FATHER KNOWS THAT YOU
NEED THESE THINGS. BUT SEEK FIRST HIS
KINGDOM, AND THESE THINGS SHALL BE
ADDED TO YOU. DO NOT BE AFRAID LITTLE
FLOCK, FOR YOUR FATHER HAS CHOSEN
GLADLY TO GIVE YOU THE KINGDOM."
LUKE 12:27-32

LETTER #7

Dear Father,

Hey, did you know that I am in New York now. Of course you did, that was silly of me. Please don't get mad at me when I say this, but I hate it, really I do. I am nine now and it seems I have been going from one adventure to another. What would I ever do without you? At five years old I asked Jesus to come into my heart and live and that's the best thing that I have ever done, because I would be so lost and heartsick and hopeless without you in my life. Today I find myself in Elmira, New York. We are living in a house on a dirty street along with about a hundred other empty, gloomy houses. You know, I used to watch Mr. Rogers on T.V. and I would give anything to disappear into the neighborhood of make believe.

I have to ask you to forgive me because Big brother and I got in trouble the other day. There is a store at the end of our street and they sell lots of good candy. At least it looks good, I have never had any money to buy any of it. Big brother and I let temptation get the best of us. We took an old can and went from door to door collecting money for some made up agency. We got a few dollars, which seemed like a million bucks and we went to the store and spent it all on candy. Don't worry, we didn't get to eat any of it, as we came out of the store there was a man standing there, that we had just collected change from and he yelled at us then took all of our candy. I am sorry. I know that this was wrong, please forgive me and my big brother. You know He is only eleven, He didn't mean to be bad, we just wanted some candy.

Big sister cut her hand up. I don't want to tell you why or you might be mad at her. I'll tell you if you will please forgive her too. She tried to break into a gumball machine at the laundry mat and it broke and cut her hand up. Other than that Father, she is a very good girl. She doesn't get into half of the trouble that brother and I do. She usually stays at home and helps mom take care of little sister.

There is a man staying at our house who is helping mom buy groceries. He is a bad man father. He slaps us and kicks us. We don't get time alone with mom anymore, he is always with her and we don't want to go near him. I don't even know his name, but big brother and I can tell you exactly what his fist look like. Oh Father, when is this whirlwind going to stop? I have written you few letters since I was born, so I have only mentioned a few of the dangers that I have been in. The ones that I haven't mentioned are like dark waves inside of me. They won't go away completely but they do come and go. I don't want to talk about all of those bad things, if that's okay with you, because I am so tired of crying. I see kids in cars or stores with their moms and dads and they are laughing and they have dolls in their buggies and they have cup cakes in their buggies and I have to be honest Father, a lot of times I wish that I were them.

I don't like this man in my house. I don't like being hit and I sure don't like seeing big brother get hit. My big brother though, will stand between me and this bad man and take a hit to protect me. Where did I get such a brother or sisters? I think that they were angels in Heaven and you sent them to me so that I would not have to go through this life alone. Thank you. Oh, Father, I haven't seen my dad in a long, long time. Where is he? What's he doing right now? I wish that he were here now instead of this angry man because my dad would never hit me, wherever he is I know that he loves me. If you could make this man quietly go away that would be fine with me. Mom doesn't know that He hits us, He told us not to tell, and we don't want to make him even madder. So if you could just quietly make him go away then she will never have to know and the rest of us will be safe. Gee, I'm doing it again aren't I? Asking for you help again. I would be dead already if it wasn't for you. I have been beaten, in a flood, in a fire, among evil men, in abandoned houses and I am still alive…only because of you. I know that I am good and I know that there are bad people in the world, I just wish that they would stop coming into my little life. I am tired Father, I am going to sleep now, I have to get my rest so that I can fight another day. I love you and I am lost in this place.

love,
your little girl

Dear daughter,

There are so many grownups that are so mad and hurt that they hurt other people. A lot of them hurt their own children or other children. This is because they don't know me or my ways. I can help them, but they don't want my help. They are so eaten up with anger and hate that everyone they know, they hurt. I am sorry that you came into the path of this angry man. I will remove him from your presence and I will not let you or your brother or sisters feel his wrath again. I love you and one day you will be strong and compassionate. You will be a protector of children and a guide for my other hurting daughters, all because of the things that you have endured. Hold on, honey, hold on tight to me and together we will step into a brighter day. Once again I remind you out of pure love that I am with you and I will never leave you.

love,
Your heavenly Father

"WHAT THE WICKED FEARS WILL COME UPON HIM, AND THE DESIRE OF THE RIGHTEOUS WILL BE GRANTED. WHEN THE WHIRLWIND PASSES, THE WICKED IS NO MORE, BUT THE RIGHTEOUS HAS AN EVERLASTING FOUNDATION."
PROVERBS 10:24-25

LETTER #8

Dear Father,

Good evening Father. I hope that you had a beautiful day today. Well I am twelve years old now. So much has happened since the last time that I wrote to you that I don't know where to start.

My family is all split up and I miss the days when I was young and those precious and few times when we were all together. I am of course talking about my dad and mom, big brother, big and little sister and me. Well things have changed again and I have to honestly say that I am not surprised in the least. Now, as I am writing to you I am living with my Father, my step mother, her children and big brother and big sister. Mom and little sister are no longer with me and my heart hurts really deeply bad. I miss my mom so bad and I worry about baby sister because she is not with me and she is not with mom. They have taken her away from all of us. A small town court system and a paid off judge took my baby sister away and placed her in the hands of a strange family. They took her from my mommy when her divorce became final with dad. Dad already had the three older kids and mom had little sister. I am not sure and I don't think that I will ever know why they took her out of my mom's arms but I can never forget the cries of my mom when this happened. The courts put little sister in a foster home, then sent a letter to my mom saying that this family wanted to adopt little sister and if my mom wanted to object to this adoption then she would have to come to the court house. At the same time they sent my mom a letter notifying her that she had a warrant for her arrest for some checks or tickets or something and that is she stepped foot into the country she would be arrested. Scared to death of going to jail and not being able to fight the adoption, my mother retained a lawyer and did not go to the courthouse. Mom had no money, so the lawyer did not argue much of a case and my mom permanently lost little sister, we all did. After that my father met his new wife and married her and now we are all living with them in our new house. We (big brother, big sister and I) call this house "the witch's hat" because it is shaped like a pointed black witch's hat. I am very torn right now Father. I know that wherever my mom is right now, she is all alone and in unspeakable pain from heartbreak. Her whole life revolved around her babies and now she hasn't got one of us with her. At the same time, my Father is doing his best to take care of us and I know that He loves us dearly too. His new wife, my step mother, is doing her very best with six kids in the house and I know that it can't be easy to throw two families together that are totally different, try to please and feed everyone and maintain ones sanity. So I feel like I am being disloyal to someone all the time because I can't please everyone by being with everyone at the same time. Now I completely understand why you say in your word that you hate divorce. Its not the people getting divorced that you hate, for you love us all no matter what and people are out there doing a lot worse things than divorce. I believe that you say this because of all the pain and confusion that it brings to the children of divorce. I don't blame my parents, they are people just like me and I make plenty of mistakes and they were fighting so much that staying together would have only hurt them more. I just wish, no, I long for those few but wonderful good ole days.

I go to a middle school now. Its terrible. The school is in an upper class neighborhood and its obvious that I am the poorest person that goes there. I don't mind being poor and doing without because this is all I know anyway, but I don't believe that I should be tormented and teased because of it. The children at my school taunt and tease me a lot, I am alone there. All of the girls are wearing pantyhose with their dresses while I wear checkered knee socks. Levis are in style, while I wear polyester pants that are too short for me. All of the girls at school have beautiful complexions and smiles, while I have pretty bad acne and oily hair. Boys never look at me and if I were to disappear from this school today no one would even notice. I am also pretty sure that I wear my sadness like a cloak about me. I cannot hide my worry for my mom and dad and my lonesome heart for little sister. Without them, my life is incomplete.

As if things weren't bad enough I have made them even worse by making a fool out of myself in front of the entire school. You see, our school put on a talent/gong show. One girl that I know has the most beautiful voice, like a bird. She was extremely shy though and wanted to enter the talent contest but not alone. Well guess who she asked? Yup, me, the only one who didn't have the heart to turn her down. Now I can't carry a tune in a bucket, so we decided that she would sing really loud and I would just whisper so that I could not be heard and she would not have to stand up there alone. Well, the day of the talent/gong show, she didn't come to school. I went to the teacher in charge of the show and he told me to find someone to take her place or do it myself. I went to my step sister, who is my age, but also is not the world's greatest singer and asked her to help me. She said no at first, but I persisted and she gave in just to get me out of a jam. We entered the large assembly with fear and trembling and we sang our hearts out. We had not been singing long at all when we heard that dreaded sound "GONG! GONG! GONG!" We left the stage with our heads hanging and our hearts in deep despair.

So, as you can imagine, if I was picked on before that day, oh how things got worse. Now every time I walk down the hall at school I hear voices yelling "GONG! GONG! GONG!" Oh Father, am I going to always be rejected by people? Am I destined to be a misfit forever? You have always told me that you have great plans for me, but really, what possible use could you have for a misfit? What plans can you have for a reject like me?

love,
your little girl

Dear daughter,

I know that divorce is hard on children. In the days of old a man stood by his wife until death. Times are changing. My people give up too easily and don't think that their marriage or families are sacred enough to fight for. I am fighting for you, though, my young one. Things will work out for your best interests, for your future. You are not a reject or a disappointment to me. I have created you just the way that I want you. How people can look at you and not see your true inner beauty disappoints me. You are indeed wonderfully made, you are beautiful, What you dress like does not matter to me and I am the one that you should worry about impressing. You impress me. You carry on and endure and you will grow to be a fine lady one day that many will look up to and admire. True beauty is the light that radiates from my children when they are full of the truth and depth of my love for them. I know that you are sad about mom and little sister, but they are also in my hands. Don't let this sadness cover your light. Let your light shine and I, yes I, the one true living God will call you beautiful. After all you are wonderfully made. Did you forget how my Son was rejected on the earth. He was a misfit too, according to the world's standards. He was not accepted either, so once again, as I have told you before, you should be honored not dismayed because you are among the best of company. Keep holding onto me and know in your heart that I love you and will always love you and that I will never, ever leave your side. You are not a reject. You are royalty. Lift your head high my daughter and walk in my light and let your true beauty be seen by this dark, cold world.

love,

Your heavenly Father, your Papa God

"ARISE, SHINE; FOR YOUR LIGHT HAS COME, AND THE GLORY OF THE LORD HAS RISEN UPON YOU. FOR BEHOLD, DARKNESS WILL COVER THE EARTH, AND DEEP DARKNESS THE PEOPLES; BUT THE LORD WILL RISE UPON YOU, AND HIS GLORY WILL APPEAR UPON YOU. AND NATIONS WILL COME TO YOUR LIGHT, AND KINGS TO THE BRIGHTNESS OF YOUR RISING."

ISAIAH 60:1-3

LETTER #9

Dear Father,

I am on the edge of thirteen, I am going to be a teenager very soon. Funny but I feel like I am about eighty years old. I can't help but have serious doubts about the rest of my life. If I am only going to be thirteen and I am already worn out and experiencing serious stress, how am I ever going to make it through the rest of my life? Father, I propose that we change the way things are going. No more yesterdays, please. I would like some sunshine and security in my tomorrows. What am I going to do when I am an adult. Who am I going to be? I have no idea. I am so used to disaster always calling the shots and then I have to go along with it and survive. I am kind of scared of being an adult and relying on myself to call all the shots. I know that this may sound strange but disaster has become a companion to me. I have almost associated comfort with disaster. I know, that's way out there, but it is also sadly true.

Well, guess where I am at now? I am in a children's home. A Presbyterian children's home. I am in this home with big brother and big sister and about one hundred and fifty other misfits and I kind of like them. How I got here is nothing less than a huge mess. We (big brother , big sister and I, no word on little sister) wanted to stay with mom. We let mom know this and so she retained a lawyer and we all went to court. The judge said no, that we needed to stay right where we were at and not move in with mom, we stood up in the court room and in a loud voice yelled "no!" Oh boy, we made the judge mad and he said that we were in contempt of court and he put us in a detention center. It's a jail for children. We were in tiny cells allowed to come out and eat and exercise then we had to be back into our cells. I was alone in my cell, no one could share cells so I didn't get to be put in with big sister. We had a super nice social worker and the first person in all of the courts and social services that really cared about our happiness. Her name was Vikkie and I will never forget her, as a matter of fact I have been wondering if maybe you sent her to us, an angel amongst the wolves. Anyway she talked to the judge and got us out of the detention center on the third day. We had come to the agreement that if we could not live with our mom, then we would not live with our dad either. It wasn't that we loved one more than the other, on the contrary, we were so tired of having to decide which one to go to and which one to hurt. No more, we were not going to decide anymore, so the courts actually honored our decision and placed us in this children's home. They said that we can stay here until we are eighteen.

So here we are. We talk and write to mom and dad and are in a state of continual apologizing to the both of them. Oh Father, it was just too much, always having to worry about breaking the heart of the parent that we weren't with, so we stuck together

on this and here we are. There are seven buildings in
this home. One is the administration and cafeteria and
three are the boys' cottages and three are the girls'
cottages. Big sister and I are in the same cottage, but
we do not share the same room. I share a room with
a girl my age. I have friends here. I also have chores
and rules to follow, but these chores and rules are my
new friends too. I lay in bed knowing what tomorrow
will be like and that's kind of cool. Now when I turn
eighteen and have to leave here I think that I will be
lost again, but Father, I like where I am at right now.
We get new clothes for school and a small allowance
for personal things. On weekends the older kids can
check the van out and we go to the movies or to
the arcade. Big sister is happy, she has a boyfriend,
big brother is happy he has a couple of girl friends.
I am not interested in boys right now. I just like to
watch T.V. in the basement or listen to music in my
room or swim. Yes, there is a pool here too. I wish
that baby sister could be here with us. Our social
worker said that she knows where she is and that the
family takes very good care of her and loves her, but
no one will love baby sister like mom and I worry
about mom a lot, because mom has a broken heart.
Mom has moved to Texas and sends us pictures of
her apartment and her cocker spaniel Max. She has a
good job and has found a good church. She is happy,
but very very lonesome for us all. Even though I am
very content here, I too am lonesome for my parents. I
hate divorce. Father, I know that you will work things
out for my family one day, but all the pain that we

have endured thus far has not vanished from my heart and even though I have no idea what my future holds I can say with total assurance that I already like it more than the past. You're gonna have to help me get over all of this one day. Right now though, I'm gonna go get some ice cream and go to the pool and enjoy this time of my life. Thanks for taking care of mom and dad for me while I'm here. You know, sometimes when I am laughing and having a good time I begin to feel guilty for enjoying myself while my parents are missing me. I guess I can't win for losing. I can't please everyone, and forgive me for my selfishness, but for just a little time I am going to please myself and enjoy the day. I love you and I think that all I need from you this time is to please stop the pain in mom and dads heart and let them know that I am truly okay where I am at and Father, would you please tell them that I still love them and will always and forever love them, but I had to take a break and love myself for a bit. I hope they understand and I thank you for always understanding…..even when I don't.

love,
your little girl

Dear daughter,

    I am glad that you are happy where you are right now. I know that this life is not perfect and I see the sadness in your heart for your parents. I am taking care of them and they are going to be fine. They are survivors, just like you. As far as your little sister, it will be a while before you see her and I know that this is another arrow in your heart, but you will be with her again one day and the wounds of the past will heal for your entire family.

Go ahead now and have a good time. I want you to be a child as long as you can. You really have not been a child yet and you were right when you said that you felt eighty because you have been through so much. Now you worry about being an adult and what will become of you when you turn eighteen and have to rely on yourself. I will still be with you when you are Eighteen, thirty eight and eighty. I don't age. I don't change. I am always your strong tower and your source of love. Situations change on you constantly, but I have not changed nor will I ever. Go ahead now and play and run and swim and yes, my daughter…go ahead and laugh. You are allowed to laugh. I love you and I am with you always… I will never, ever leave you nor forsake you.

love,
Your Father, your pappa God

"TO GRANT THOSE WHO MOURN IN ZION,
GIVING THEM A GARLAND INSTEAD OF
ASHSES, THE OIL OF GLADNESS INSTEAD
OF MOURNING, THE MANTLE OF PRAISE
INSTEAD OF A SPIRIT OF FAINTING."
ISAIAH 61:3

LETTER #10....

Dear Father,

Hello there, my sweet Father. I love you. I am doing really well right now. I am writing you a letter for the first time that contains no real tragedy. I am writing to thank you for how my life is going right now. I am in Texas with mom now. I am fourteen years old. Big sister was already here and big brother will be arriving next week. I told a fib at the start of this letter. There is one tragedy that I have to mention. Little sister is not here, nor is she coming. We hear word that she is doing really good and is happy and healthy, but how can one be totally happy when torn away from their bloodline? I hope that she really is happy and I hope that she remembers me. I hope that she remembers mom and how much mom loves her and may she one day know how broken moms heart is over their separation. I pray that one day she will know the truth and that this side of her family (her real family) never for a second wanted to let her go but that she was literally torn from our arms. Father, could you tell her that we love her, miss her, want her with us and will always hold her dear as our baby sister? Dad is still in Virginia and I believe that he is happy with my step mother. Bless them with happiness and peace. You see, I just want everyone to be happy, like me.

Well, I am here in Texas with mom. I remember when I got off of the plane last week and the heat hit me like a sheet of hot coals. It literally took my breath away. I don't know what I was really expecting from Texas, maybe oil wells and cowboys, but I got heat and mosquitoes. That is all fine with me because MOM was waiting for me when I got off that plane. Mom has a very nice home, it feels safe and secure here and I really like that. She goes to a fine church that really cares about her and she has a good job as a secretary at a brick yard. Her boss, at the brickyard seems to be a very nice man and he goes to the same church that we do. I think that he likes mom and I'll bet that they start dating soon. It's okay with me if she dates, I just want her to be happy. I'll say it again, all I want, all that I ever wanted, all that I will ever want is for everyone to be happy. Big brother should be arriving next week and we will venture out on our new life in Texas. Thank you Father, thank you that I have a little peace for once. I really needed it. I love you.

love,
your little girl

Dear daughter,
   You are right where I want you. I am glad that you are happy. I want you to be happy and its very okay for you to smile once in a while. I will let your baby sister know that she is loved by you and your family. I am keeping her safe within my arms. I love you…. enjoy! Love, Pappa God

"BLESSED IS THE MAN WHO TRUSTS IN THE LORD AND WHOSE TRUST IS THE LORD. FOR HE WILL BE LIKE A TREE PLANTED BY THE WATER, THAT EXTENDS ITS ROOTS BY THE STREAM AND WILL NOT FEAR WHEN THE HEAT COMES; BUT ITS LEAVES WILL BE GREEN, AND IT WILL NOT BE ANXIOUS IN A YEAR OF DROUGHT NOR CEASE TO YIELD FRUIT."

JEREMIAH 17:7-8

LETTER #11

Dear Father,

Hi Father. This is probably my last letter to you and I don't even know if you are reading this. You probably looked and saw who it was from and threw it away. I have really messed up this time and I have been told that You, yes, even you, my life long companion, has had enough of me and that you just can't forgive me this one. It's alright. You have helped me so much when I was little. You have rescued me so many times from my own personal failures. I guess that you have a container of mercy with each humans name on it and mine is all used up. I don't blame you Father. I am a bad mess and a lost cause and pretty filthy I would rather you not look at me anyway.

I am fifteen now, almost sixteen. I am still with mom in Texas. She married her boss from the brickyard and he is very good to all of us (big brother, big sister, me and mom). He has built a beautiful home in the country for all of us and we have a little pond in front of it and it's a peaceful, safe place to live and I thank you. We still go to the same church that mom was going to when I first came to Texas. They started a Christian school here for the children of the congregation and then comes the bad part. We all go to the Christian school and the people are real nice. You can see the joy and peace in all of the faces. I am the one that made the mistake.

Two weeks ago a carnival came to town. I went there with several of my friends from church. There was a guy about seventeen running one of the rides he was very handsome. He liked me and gave me a bunch of free rides. I went back the next day with some friends and that guy saw me and asked me if I would come back later that night after they close down and spend some time with him. My friends said, "no, don't do it, he is pure trouble." I didn't listen to them and I snuck back up there later that night and met with him. I don't know why I did it, or what drew me to this boy but I slept with him that night. I have given up a sacred part of myself to that stranger and I hated him immediately afterwards and I went home crying, full of emptiness and self-loathing. I told no one, except my very best friend at school and she promised not to tell a soul. The very next day I was called into the pastors office and they told me that they were aware that I committed fornication and that I was bragging about it to the other students. Not so, I only told one person, and I guess the reason that I told her was that I had to confess to someone. It was decided among the pastor and his elders that if I went through an exorcism and apologized to the entire school for bringing the sin of fornication into the school then I could remain a student. I did as I was told.

First came the exorcism. The pastor's wife and a few other women took me to a house and sat me in a chair in the middle of the living room and started casting out spirits. Funny, I never felt anything weird

inside of me, just embarrassment. I sat there and wept
and that was about it. I don't' know what they were
expecting maybe my head turning backwards or split
pea soup throw up or maybe a weird voice coming
from somewhere inside of me, but I guess that I
disappointed them, because I just sat there and wept,
I was so embarrassed. Next came the confession in
front of the whole school. The school was called
together to assemble on my behalf and I was asked to
come up front of the room. I told them all that I was
sorry for what I had done and sorry that I brought that
"fornication spirit" into the school. That was really
hard to do, but it wasn't the hardest thing that I had
to do. You see that was yesterday. Today I had to do
something even harder. At lunch time we are allowed
to leave the school so I walked off the school property
and out of sight (so I thought) and smoked a cigarette.
Yes father, I smoke too. Anyway while I was sitting
in a parking lot smoking, one of the elders drove by
and saw me, this caused my final expulsion from
the school. They all knew that I smoked, so I don't
understand. When I went back to school after lunch
I was summoned out of my classroom back to the
pastor's office. It was obvious to them that I did not
regret my sin and therefore did not truly repent and
that I would have to leave the premises immediately.
Now came the hardest thing that I had to do…call my
mom to have her come and pick me up. Oh Father, I
did not want to do this. This was her church that she
brought me into, her friends and Oh Father I did not
want to let her down. I called her and told her the

entire story and waited for the silence on the other end of the phone to break. Finally she spoke. Mom spoke the only comforting words that I had heard in many a day. She said "oh honey, I can't believe that they did that to you. God has forgiven you and so have I, this is wrong of them and Hold on tight, I will be right there." Good ole mom, none can compare to her, no one, ever! After I hung up with her I told them that she was on her way, They said that I could not return to the classroom to get my things and that I needed to leave right now. I will never forget their last words as I walked out of the pastor's office…the pastor looked directly into my eyes and said "you belong to the devil and you will become a witch or a whore for him and that is your future." That was it. His final words of wisdom…the curse bestowed upon me by this man who was so great in my eyes.

I am now sitting outside on the front steps of the church/school waiting for mom. I guess that this is goodbye Father. This pastor and these elders are men of God. What they speak must be the truth. Surely they prayed before they made this decision and prayer is communication with you, so this must also be your decision. I won't really miss the school, I will miss my friends, but Father, most of all I am really going to miss you. What am I ever going to do without you. You have been my protection, my hero, the love of my life, my comfort and you have been my best friend. I will be lost without you and I don't want to let you go. I regret, no I hate the night I went to the carnival. I don't know why I did it, but it was a lethal

mistake. I have lost you and I am in deep regret. I
have become empty. I have to let go of your hand
and that is something that I have never done before,
something that I thought I would never have to do,
but now I let go and I walk away from you. For I have
become filthy and I cannot impose my filthiness on
your Holiness. Goodbye my love…..goodbye.

love,
your little girl

Dear daughter,

Listen to me…Don't turn your back on me. I did
not let you go. Sometimes the enemy will use my
word and even my people to hurt one of my sheep.
These men did not seek my will in this, they acted
upon fear. Fear for their own children. One day you
will have to forgive them for this and that's gonna be
hard for you. Right now though, it's very important
for you to know that I heard your repentance and
I have forgiven you already. I love you. So many
times I have told you that I will never, ever leave
you or forsake you, I still mean this, there is nothing
that You, or any of my children can do to make me
turn my back on you. Your sin is not unforgivable. I
forgive you. You are my daughter. The enemy wants
you to walk away from me. He has deceived you
making you think that I have sent you away, this is
not true. I will never send you away. Can you hear
me honey? Are you listening to my voice or has
despair and shame made deaf your ears from my
voice? You must hear me now, or you have a very

rough road ahead of you. I still love you. My love is unconditional…I simply love you.

love,

Your heavenly Father, your Papa God

"BE GRACIOUS TO ME, O GOD, ACCORDING TO THY LOVINGKINDNESS ACCORDING TO THE GREATNESS OF THY COMPASSION BLOT OUT MY TRANSGRESSIONS. WASH ME THOROUGHLY FROM MY INIQUITY, AND CLEANSE ME FROM MY SIN. FOR I KNOW MY TRANSGRESSIONS, AND MY SIN IS EVER BEFORE ME. AGAINST THEE, THEE ONLY, I HAVE SINNED AND DONE WHAT IS EVIL IN THY SIGHT, SO THAT THOU ART JUSTIFIED WHEN THOU DOST SPEAK, AND BLAMELESS WHEN THOU DOST JUDGE, BEHOLD, THOU DOST DESIRE TRUTH IN THE INNERMOST BEING, AND IN THE HIDDEN PART THOU WILT MAKE ME KNOW WISDOM. PURIFY ME WITH HYSSOP, AND I SHALL BE CLEAN; WASH ME, AND I SHALL BE WHITER THAN SNOW. MAKE ME TO HEAR JOY AND GLADNESS, HIDE THY FACE FROM MY SINS, AND BLOT OUT ALL MY INIQUITIES. CREATE IN ME A CLEAN HEART, O GOD, AND RENEW A STEAD FAST SPIRIT WITHIN ME. DO NOT CAST ME AWAY FROM THY PRESENCE, AND DO NOT TAKE THY HOLY SPIRIT FROM ME. RESTORE TO ME THE JOY OF THY SALVATION; AND SUSTAIN ME WITH A WILLING SPIRIT.

THEN I WILL TEACH TRANSGRESSORS THY WAYS, AND SINNERS WILL BE CONVERTED TO ME."

PSALMS 51:1-13

"BUT WHEN THEY PERSISTED IN ASKING JESUS, HE STRAIGHTENED UP AND SAID TO THEM 'HE WHO IS WITHOUT SIN AMONG YOU, LET HIM BE THE FIRST TO THROW A STONE AT HER'."

JOHN 8:7

LETTER #12

Dear Father,

Help me! Please, please Help me! I am so lost. I am surrounded by such a darkness that I cannot even see my self anymore. I am twenty years old now and I am very, very desperate. I know that I have not talked to you in a very long time. I don't even know if you want to talk to me now, but Father I am so scared and so alone. I am all alone in this big world and I have not been doing a very good job of taking care of myself. I live in bars and sleep in motels. My breakfast is tequila and my supper is whiskey. I am skin and bones and I am all used up. The only company that I get is the occasional one night stand that is gone by the time I wake up and I am nothing more than trash. I look in the mirror and what I see is hideous and dead. I have not seen family in a long long time. I don't call mom or dad because I have nothing good about myself to say and I don't want to lie to them and tell them that everything is okay. I don't call brother or sister because I don't have the courage to tell them that I am a homeless drunk that hasn't a dime or a hope. I borrow, beg and steal enough money to get a room every night and have been fortunate to have not had to sleep on the streets. I'll go home with people that feel sorry for me or just want to use me and I don't care. I remember that dreadful day when I was told that my life would take this course, you know that day my sin was found out and I was kicked out of the church and out of your presence. Oh, but Father I need you so badly. I am right now in a motel room. It is eleven A.M., one hour before check out time. I don't even have a dollar. I can't remember who brought me here, but they are gone now. I am so hungry and in one hour I will be walking out this door and onto the streets. I can't go on like this. Send me an angel, send me a word, send me a sign that I am still your little girl. I have missed you so bad and have been going from misery to misery searching for the impossible. I have been trying to fill that void that was created when I walked away from you five years ago. Did I walk away or did you walk away? I thought I heard you say one day that you did forgive me, was I hearing things? Were my hopes invading my thought life? Have you really forgiven me? Oh God in Heaven, I am very aware of your purity and Holiness and of my sin and filthiness and I have to ask "am I fixable?"

I have fallen so far, will I ever get out? I have ruined the little girl that I was, can I ever be cleaned up? Oh Father, where will I go from here? Will I be sleeping under a bridge tonight? Will I still be alive tomorrow? I hope so, because if I died today I would burn in hell for all of my sins. You see, I'm not your sweet, innocent little girl anymore.

I miss her…the me that I used to be. Where did I go? Where am I going today? Help me Mighty God… please, please…help me.

love,
your lost little girl

Dear daughter,

Here I am…right where I have been all along. I have been calling you and trying time after time to get your attention, but you keep turning a deaf ear towards me. I have never left you. You walked away from our relationship. It's time to come back, honey. This is your lowest point thus far and it is time to get back up and become the you that I have created you to be. Hold on, I am sending help as I always have. You see, by "world" standards you should have been dead already….diseases, murdered or self destruction, but I have been with you the whole way, sending my warring soldiers to fight for you and protect you. The enemy has been after your destruction since the day you were born, but I have not let that happen. I have great and mighty plans for you honey, or have you forgotten our letters of long ago?

I am right here and I am so glad that you have finally acknowledged my presence again, now when I have lifted you out of this danger will come a long and magnificent time of healing, so hold on honey, help is on the way.

love,
your Papa God, your Father

"INDEED, WE HAD THE SENTENCE OF DEATH WITHIN OURSELVES IN ORDER THAT WE SHOULD NOT TRUST IN OURSELVES, BUT IN GOD WHO REAISES THE DEAD; WHO DELIVERED US FROM SO GREAT A PERIL OF

DEATH, AND WILL DELIVER US, HE ON WHOM
WE HAVE SET OUR HOPE, AND HE WILL YET
DELIVER US."
II CORINTHIANS 1:9-10

LETTER #13

Dear Father,

Good afternoon Father. I have some news for you. I have just gotten married. I am twenty two now and although my life is still a major mess I think the winds of change are going to blow my way very soon. I met someone and I married him. When I met him, he was rough and tough, but I saw a gentleness inside of him and I knew that beyond that rough exterior lives a gentle giant. Let me explain…

I was bartending in a hole in the wall place. Just some small dark corner of the world where I was hidden snugly away from reality. I was alone. I was and still am a very lost sheep. One day this big rowdy looking man came up to me and said "if you ever need any help, I will help you." I didn't know him or anything about him, but I took him up on his offer. I told him that I was alone, living out of a suitcase and very tired of the path that I was on. He took me to his home, treated me with respect, like a real gentleman. He never made a pass at me or anything. He had a son, four years old, a blonde haired, blue-eyed sweet little angel. Now it was the second day that I was there that I knew this was the man that I would marry. I knew this for two reasons.

The first reason was our conversation we had while at the park walking around. He began to tell me about his grandma. Where she lives, what she is like, how much she means to him and how wonderful she is to him. As he talked about her I saw a tenderness in his big blue eyes. I heard a quiet honor for her in his deep voice. He held her in high esteem. I saw how much this man loved his grandma and I just knew then that he would love me the same way one day. The second reason I knew that this man was part of my future was because of his little boy. This tender, sweet child came to me on the second day that I knew him and looked up into my eyes and asked "are you going to be my new mommy? Because I would like that." When he spoke those words to me I realized that he saw the goodness in me that I had long since abandoned. He saw hope and security in me that I had no idea even existed. He had faith in me and it shook my heart because I did not see such faith in me. For these two reasons I knew that this was to be my family.

We married a few months after that. We are now struggling from day to day. Some days we eat some we don't. There were even a few days that we had to sleep in our car, but at least the three of us were together and that began to change the whole picture for me. One day I had decided that I wanted a real life. No more drinking or going hungry. I wanted an address and a life and I wanted my new little step son to have a real yard to play in. I told my new husband that I refused to live this way anymore and that I was going to walk away from this life style immediately and he could either walk away with me or stay on the road to nowhere. I then went to a motel room and told

him where I was going. I told him that if he wanted
to make a new life with me then to come knock on
my door and that would begin a new day for us, but
if he wanted to continue to party and waste another
precious day of life to not bother to come. I wasn't at
the motel room three hours when there came a knock
on the door. When I opened the door, there they stood,
one blue eyed gentle giant with tears in his eyes and
one small sweet blue eyed angel with a huge smile on
his face. Thus our new life begins.

We have now gotten our first apartment together.
We started out with a blanket and a couple of pillows.
We now have a T.V. and sofa too and there is a little
food in the fridge. We are gonna make it father,
because I believe that you have your hand in this.
I believe that this is all part of your plan. I can't
imagine what my life will be like in ten years when I
have been married for just as long and my step son is
fourteen, but I have this fresh and incredible feeling
that everything is going to be better. I know that this
is because for the first time in six very long years that
I have done something that you wanted me to do. I
feel your approval in this and I can see you smiling
down on me and my new little family right now. I
can even see a small part of the old me, that was
your sweet, trusting, innocent little girl and I like that
feeling. Thank you for sending me not one but two
angels. One: a blue-eyed gentle giant and the other: a
small fair haired, blue-eyed, precious cherub. Thank
you Father, for not forgetting your plans for me and
for (in spite of myself) carrying those plans through. I

have missed you, but I feel that our time of separation is about to come to an end. You are my rock and my never ending source of encouragement. I have always and will always love you.

love,
your little girl

Dear daughter,

Congratulations on your new marriage. Marriage is a sacred thing to me, treat your husband with love and respect and treat your new little boy with love and protect him, for you are also his angel. They need you as badly as you need them, so I put the three of you together. Now, all you need is more of me. I am not finished with you, and desire a lot more of you, so be prepared for times of growing, learning and healing. I bless you and your marriage and may your love multiply in many ways.

love,
your heavenly Father

"FOR I AM CONFIDENT OF THIS VERY THING, THAT HE WHO BEGAN A NEW WORK IN YOU WILL PERFECT IT UNTIL THE DAY OF CHRIST JESUS."
PHILIPPIANS 1:6

LETTER #14.......

Dear Father,

We have just moved into our first house. Wow!
A real house, with a real front and back yard. For the
first time, maybe the first time ever, I have a place to
rest my head where I feel perfectly safe. I am twenty
five years old now. My son (of course he is really my
step son, but he and I don't feel that way, I feel as if I
gave birth to him) anyway he is now nine years old.
He is very precious and gentle, he is such a good boy.
My husband has been working for the same company
three years now and is doing very well. I am working
part time also. We have really straightened up a lot
Father, I think that you have probably noticed this.
We don't drink or hang out with anyone who lives
that "partying" lifestyle. As a matter of fact we kind
of keep to ourselves and enjoy our new home and
its privacy. There is one thing about our new house
that is kind of unsettling for me though. Right behind
our house, I mean ten feet away from our backyard
is a church. I don't know why it bothers me, it's as
if it knows I am here and kind of calls me or haunts
me. Now Father, you know that I have not set foot
in a church since I was kicked out of that Christian
school. I have done some growing up since then, but
really Father, between then and now I committed a
lot of sins. I am really filthy now and I know that if I
tried to go to a church they would be able to look at

me and see all of my many former sins and would not welcome me. I don't think that I could take rejection like that again. Not from your people, not from you sanctuary…not from you…I mean…if it really was you in the first place that cast me out. Anyway I just can't make myself walk over there, but I do miss you.

Father, I miss you. I miss being around a lot of people that love you as I do. I miss holding my hands up to you in praise. I miss walking into a place and your love is so strong there that it overwhelms me and I melt into a mass of tears and speechlessness. Oh Father, where would I be today, if that dreadful day ten years ago had never happened? I might have been a preacher or a missionary like my parents, but instead I am doing good to not cuss, or drink and to occasionally talk to you. After all that I have done, are you even listening to me? How could you even care about a low life like me anyway? How many times do I even dare to ask you for forgiveness? How many times do you forgive? Well, I guess that I will end this letter now, there's not much sense in writing a lot, if you probably won't even open it, not when you see who it's from. I love you though and I don't blame you for classifying me as useless. I am still gonna love you though and I can't control this longing for you in my life again. I miss you Father…I really miss you.

love,
your "lonesome for you" daughter

Dear daughter,

How can you think that I don't love you? How can you think that I am not listening every time you speak? Who do you think gave you the strength to walk away from that deadly life style? Who do you think got you into that house when you had no credit or even a checking account? And why do you think that there is a church in your backyard? It's gonna take you a little while to see what I am trying to tell you. This is what I want you to know…I have put you right by that church because I am calling you back to me. I know that you miss me, but multiply that by a thousand times then you will know how much I miss you. I love you so much that I placed you into this house to get you into that church to get you back into my arms, where, by the way, you belong.

You say that the church there kind of bothers you. This is why. I have sent my Spirit to call you, to woo you, to beckon you back to me. You can't get this church off your mind, can you? Well, be prepared because this church is going to "bother" you everyday until you realize that its not the church at all, but that it's me, trying to get you back on the right track and back into my will for you. You end your letter by expressing that you doubt if I have forgiven you. I know that road you have been down. I know every deed that you have done. I have also heard your apology. You have stepped out of that life style and when you turn your back on sin, that my daughter is called repentance. I have forgiven you each and every time you have asked me to. You are forgiven, honey.

You are forgiven and by the way, I never run out of forgiveness. This is who I am. I am forgiveness, I am mercy...Honey...I am love.

Love,
your awaiting Father God

"AND WHEN YOU WERE DEAD IN YOUR TRANSGRESSIONS AND THE UNCIRCUMCISION OF YOUR FLESH, HE MADE YOU ALIVE TOGETHER WITH HIM, HAVING FORGIVEN US ALL OUR TRANSGRESSIONS, HAVING CANCELED OUT OUR CERTIFICATE OF DEBT AND CONSISTING OF DECREES AGAINST US AND WHICH WAS HOSTILE TO US; AND HE HAS TAKEN IT OUT OF THE WAY, HAVING NAILED IT TO THE CROSS."
COLOSSIANS 2:13-14

"BLESS THE LORD, O MY SOUL; AND ALL THAT IS WITHIN ME, BLESS HIS HOLY NAME, BLESS THE LORD, O MY SOUL, AND FORGET NONE OF HIS BENEFITS; WHO PARDONS ALL YOUR INIQUITIES; WHO HEALS ALL OF YOUR DISEASES; WHO REDEEMS YOUR LIFE FROM THE PIT; WHO CROWNS YOU WITH LOVING-KINDNESS AND COMPASSION; WHO SATISFIES YOUR YEARS WITH GOOD THINGS, SO THAT YOUR YOUTH IS RENEWED LIKE THE EAGLE."
PSALMS 103:1-5

LETTER #15...

Dear Father,

I am home! I am back in your arms! Here I am Lord, Here I am! I can't believe that you welcomed me back with open arms. All this time, all these years I thought that you didn't want me anymore. I thought that I was an unforgivable being and now you have simply and wonderfully taken my breath away when you said "welcome home my child." I can breath again. I can hope again. I can dream again. I think that I can even take my tail out from between my legs and look people in the eye again. All because you have looked upon me and smiled.

I have been in this house a year with the church behind me always catching my eye, always on my mind. I have come so close so many times to walking over there and walking in, but the knowledge of my filthiness was too much and I could never do it. That is not until three days ago. You see, the church put a huge tent up and put a sign up that said 'tent revival every night this week.' The first night that the revival started I was sitting out on my porch and I could hear the music and the singing. I even edged over by the side of my house to listen closer and then I wept. Oh how I wept. I used to sing to you that way. I used to join in the lifting of hands to you and I missed it immensely. The next night, I intentionally sat on the porch to listen. "That's it!" I said to my little blue-

eyed son. "I have to go over there." I told him and he
gladly said that he would go with me. My husband
was not interested in the least. So JJ and I walked
over there. I sat in the back row under the big tent.
Just as I sat in the chair I began to cry. Your love was
so overwhelming that I could not contain myself. I
cried and cried. For the first time in eleven years I
felt like I belonged where I was. As I cried I heard
you say that not only did you love me, not only have
you forgiven me, but that you had been missing me as
well.

The worship team began to sing Amazing Grace,
and I stood and lifted my hands to you, thanking you
with all that was within me, for your Grace that you
have given towards me. I was clean. No more filth.
I was white as snow at that very precious moment.
Clean, Father, really clean. I was no longer trash
in my eyes, because you gently told me, that I was
NEVER trash in your eyes. I have re-dedicated my
life to you. I have repented of all of my many, many
former sins. I have become a new creation. I have
just stepped back into your will and your wonderful,
healing light. Jesus, would you please come back into
my heart and stay there. I won't ever do anything
again to make myself turn my back on you. You never
left did you? No, it was me, I was the one that walked
away, so now I walk back into your loving arms. I am
home Father....I am here, right here....with you.

love,
your prodigal daughter

Dear daughter,

Welcome back honey…welcome back. We are celebrating your return in Heaven right now. What a celebration it is, and it's all for you, because I have been waiting so long for you to come home. It does not matter where you have been or what you have been doing. All that matters is that you are back home, in my arms where you belong. You are back in my will and among those that will guide you and love you as well. Welcome back honey.

Love,
your celebrating Father

"A CERTAIN MAN HAD TWO SONS: AND THE YOUNGER OF THEM SAID TO HIS FATHER "FATHER, GIVE ME THE SHARE OF THE ESTATE THAT FALLS TO ME." AND HE DIVIDED HIS WEALTH BETWEEN THEM. AND NOT MANY DAYS LATER, THE YOUNGER SON GATHERED EVERYTHING TOGETHER AND WENT ON A JOURNEY INTO A DISTANT COUNTRY, AND THERE HE SQUANDERED HIS ESTATE WITH LOOSE LIVING. NOW, WHEN HE HAD SPENT EVERYTHING, A SEVERE FAMINE OCCURRED IN THAT COUNTRY, AND HE BEGAN TO BE IN NEED. AND HE WENT AND ATTACHED HIMSELF TO ONE OF THE CITIZENS OF THAT COUNTRY, AND HE SENT HIM INTO THE FIELDS TO FEED SWINE. AND HE WAS LONGING TO FILL HIS STOMACH WITH THE PODS THAT THE SWINE

WERE EATING, AND NO ONE WAS GIVING
ANYTHING TO HIM. BUT WHEN HE CAME
TO HIS SENSES, HE SAID "HOW MANY OF
MY FATHERS HIRED MEN HAVE MORE THAN
ENOUGH BREAD, AND I AM DYING HERE
WITH HUNGER! I WILL GET UP AND GO TO
MY FATHER, AND WILL SAY TO HIM 'FATHER,
I HAVE SINNED AGAINST HEAVEN, AND IN
YOUR SIGHT; I AM NO LONGER WORTHY TO
BE CALLED YOUR SON; MAKE ME AS ONE
OF YOUR HIRED MEN." AND HE GOT UP AND
CAME TO HIS FATHER. BUT WHILE HE WAS
STILL A LONG WAY OFF, HIS FATHER SAW
HIM, AND FELT COMPASSION FOR HIM, AND
RAN AND EMBRACED HIM AND KISSED HIM.
AND THE SON SAID TO HIM, "FATHER, I HAVE
SINNED AGAINST HEAVEN AND IN YOUR
SIGHT; I AM NO LONGER WORTHY TO BE
CALLED YOUR SON." BUT THE FATHER SAID
TO HIS SLAVES "QUICKLY BRING OUT THE
BEST ROBE AND PUT IT ON HIM, AND PUT A
RING ON HIS HAND AND SANDALS ON HIS
FEET; AND BRING THE FATTENED CALF, KILL
IT, AND LET US EAT AND BE MERRY; FOR THIS
SON OF MINE WAS DEAD, AND HAS COME
TO LIFE AGAIN, AND HE WAS LOST; AND
HAS BEEN FOUND.' AND THEY BEGAN TO BE
MERRY."

LUKE 15:11-24

LETTER #16....

Dear Father,

    I have exhausted our money and I have been to several different doctors, including a fertility specialist. It seems that I can't have children. Oh I know that I have JJ and he is indeed my son. I wanted to experience pregnancy, feel a life within me and I wanted to know what a baby would look like if it came from me. I love JJ and want to give him brothers or sisters or both. Lord, I want to have a baby some day but I am beginning to lose hope. I have not been attending the church regularly, you know, the one in my back yard. I thought about going over there and asking them to pray for me. The specialist that I went to did not say that I couldn't have babies, but our insurance doesn't cover this and it is going to be very expensive to undergo tests. Because my husband has JJ, I know that it is not him, so that leaves me doesn't it? I want a baby so bad Father, but only you can take it from here. There's no more money for doctors and I am twenty five years old and never been pregnant. Not looking so good huh? Anyway I am feeling kind of down and once again approaching you with one of my problems. I ask now, Father, in the name of Jesus, would you please bless me with a child? please?

love,
your little girl

Dear daughter,

I am happy that you love your little step son as your own. However, you need to remember the shape that your lives were in when you got married. You could barely feed one child. You were homeless on more than one occasion. How could you have taken care of two or three children then? Finally you are beginning to settle down and have a normal life. I have heard your cry. I am faithful and true. Trust in me, believe in my greatness and power and then sit back and let me be God.

love,
your pappa God

"AND WHATEVER YOU ASK IN MY NAME,
THAT I WILL DO, THAT THE FATHER MAY
BE GLORIFIED IN THE SON, IF YOU ASK ME
ANYTHING IN MY NAME I WILL DO IT."
JOHN 14:13-14

"AND JESUS ANSWERED SAYING TO THEM
'HAVE FAITH IN GOD.'"
MARK 11:22

LETTER #17....

Dear Father,

I wanted to let you know about a special group of people. I wanted to let you know that I have found a true church. A group of people that love very unconditionally, that do not judge and that accept people just the way they are. I have found a church home. Of course it is the church in my backyard. It has a name though 'Houston N.W. Foursquare Church' also known as 'Life Church'. What a precious group of people. You see, since that day of the tent revival, I have only gone into the church a few times. When I did go, I would sit in the very back and hold my head down and run out as soon as the service was over. The last time that I did that, as I was trying to slide out the door a woman came up to me and introduced herself to me, then she did something really amazing. She hugged me and said "I love with Jesus' love." I couldn't believe it! We talked for a few minutes and then her husband came up and shook my hand and began talking to me. They talked to me as if I was an old friend or even family. I went back the next Sunday and this couple began introducing me around to the other members of the church. Everyone was hugging me and saying that they Love me in the Lord. They didn't know me, so how could they love me? If they did know the things that I have done they would not love me....would they? Well that is what

I was thinking, but Sunday after Sunday I went back and made friends and found out a beautiful truth. The church is full of people with ugly pasts. Ex-druggies, adulterers, used to be drinkers, the church is full of sinners, just like me. Just like me, at one point they decided they couldn't go on that way and came to you for help. They have all been delivered, healed and born again. Before I found this body of believers I thought that the church was full of perfect people that had their noses so high in the air that they would drown if it rained. I didn't know that church people made mistakes, must less confessed it. This is so cool Lord. So very, very cool. I belong with these people because I am imperfect just like them, but striving to be a better child for you. Oh and these people love you very much. I know this, because of the way that they loved me right out the gate, and as they got to know me and some of the mistakes that I have made along the way they didn't turn their backs on me…Oh Father, they loved me even more for it. Now that is the way that you are and have been all of my life. I was always the one thinking that you didn't want anything to do with me anymore and yet you loved me and loved me and you still do. I have confessed and repented of every ugly sin that I have committed in my life and you love me. This body takes on your characteristics and by their fruit I know that I have found true Christians (followers of Christ). I wanted to tell you that I appreciate you. I know now why we got into this house…because you love me. You loved me so much that you put me in a house right beside a church. Thank you Father. Also, as we both know I need to thank you for something else. For my children. I am now pregnant for the second time and I know it's a boy again. I have three sons, and how can I ever thank you enough? You are so good to me, You are my God, my sweet, powerful pappa God and I love you tenderly and deeply. Oh Father, I can remember when I was six years old and had the whole playground singing "JESUS LOVES ME," and that is how I feel now. Back in contact with you…no even better. I have a personal relationship with you again. I can remember when I was fifteen, before I sinned and was kicked out of the church, yes I remember the day that you baptized me in your Holy Spirit and I was hearing your voice and sharing your word with others. That is how I feel now and it feels so right. You complete me and all that I am. You are my life, my everything and I was so empty and lost without you. I don't ever want to step out of our relationship again. I don't ever, ever want to walk away from you again. I am so in love with you. You are the lifter of my head and the lover of my soul and you are my dearest treasure. I love you Father, your little girl loves your dearly.

love,
your little girl

Dear daughter,

I know that you love me. Life can be really hard and can harden hearts and make ears deaf to me. Circumstance, the enemy and your own selves fight me constantly and all I want from any of my children is to have a personal relationship with them. I just want to love on my children until they overflow with my presence and glory. I have been chasing you down for a long time and even if today you were still out of my will, I would still be chasing you. Why? Simply because I love you. I want to tell something that is very important…I want you to thank your mom and your dad. You see, the entire time that you were out there in the dark and straying farther and farther from me, they were praying for you. It's the praying parents that really get my attention because they are so persistent and constant in their prayers for their children. Thank them for their faithful prayers on your behalf. I love you and it is not going to be easy street from now on. As a matter of fact the enemy has now taken notice of you again and is out to kill, steal and destroy you and yours. However, I have given you my Son who defeated the enemy two thousand years ago, now all that you must do is to walk in that victory. Have faith in me and walk in knowledge of all that my Son accomplished on the cross and you will be fine.

love,
Your Heavenly Father

"THEREFORE THE LORD LONGS TO BE GRACIOUS TO YOU, AND THEREFORE HE WAITS ON HIGH TO HAVE COMPASSION ON YOU. FOR THE LORD IS A GOD JUSTICE; HOW BLESSED ARE ALL THOSE WHO LONG FOR

HIM. O PEOPLE IN ZION, INHABITANT IN
JERUSALEM, YOU WILL WEEP NO LONGER.
HE WILL SURELY BE GRACIOUS TO YOU AT
THE SOUND OF YOUR CRY; WHEN HE HEARS
IT, HE WILL ANSWER YOU. ALTHOUGH
THE LORD HAS GIVEN YOU THE BREAD OF
PRIVATION AND WATER OF OPPRESSION,
HE YOUR TEACHER WILL NO LONGER HIDE
HIMSELF, BUT YOUR EYES WILL BEHOLD
YOUR TEACHER, AND YOUR EARS WILL
HEAR A WORD BEHIND YOU, "THIS IS THE
WAY, WALK IN IT," WHENEVER YOU TURN TO
THE RIGHT OR THE LEFT."
                    ISAIAH 30:18-21

LETTER #18......

Dear Father,

As I am writing this I am so full of emotions, feelings and thoughts that I am overwhelmed, but for the good. I am resting my head on a pillow as I am gazing out of the window of a passenger van. I am surrounded by some of the most beautiful and gracious women that I have ever known. These are my sisters in the Lord. We are on our way home from Tulsa where we had just spent four awesome days in your presence at the Foursquare International Women's Convention. Oh Father I have been in your sweet presence the entire time and I don't ever want this precious time together to end. I want to take your presence with me as I go home to my Husband and three precious sons. I know that they are waiting eagerly for my return. It was so hard to leave them for four days, but I am married to a good man and a good daddy and he has taken very good care of my babies and we have talked twice a day while I have been gone. I will not be the same wife or mother that left four days ago. I am forever changed. You have lifted my head, healed me, restored unto me what was mine all along and you have equipped me to go forward and minister to others. Yes, you did all of this in four short days, but I know that the last several years of my life have led up to this moment in time when you reached into my innermost being and touched my

heart with your Holy, healing hand. From the moment
that we stepped into the coliseum your presence
overwhelmed all of us and you moved in mighty and
unforgettable ways. It was in one of the classes that
I chose to take that things became personal. I wanted
to take a class on prophecy and as I walked into the
room of about a hundred women I knew that you
were there waiting. I was sitting in my chair and our
speaker was full of your spirit and she said, "There
are some women here who have been hurt by the
church and the Lord wants to take that hurt out of you
right now." I began to cry as I walked forward with
about twenty other women. Our speaker was on the
other end of the line of weeping women when I began
to laugh. I couldn't control it and I laughed hard and
loud. Then I heard other laughing as I slowly fell to
the floor. I don't think that this precious woman ever
even made it over to me, but you did, didn't you?
You took that deep, deep scar and totally removed it
from me in that exact moment. The laughter roared
out of me, I guess because the healing was so deep
and intense that my physical being could only laugh.
I must have laid there for ten minutes laughing
along with five or six other women who must have
really been hurt like me. Finally, after gaining my
composure I returned to my seat. It was then that
You spoke to me through this obedient speaker as she
looked at me and said that you wanted me to know
that You would return to me the years that the locusts
had stripped away. I knew what that meant. I knew
that at fifteen years old I was headed very quickly into

your perfect will for my life but I fell into a trap and lost all of those years, just lost them. Now though, You have said that you would return those years to me. You have not let your plans for me go, despite myself or losses. You had a plan for me ever since I was in my mother's womb and you were not gonna let the enemy or time change your plans for me. Wow! I am sitting here in a sort of shock, a good kind of shock. As if that wasn't enough to comprehend, now as I am resting my head on a pillow and gazing out at the road you are telling me to remember these last four days because this is what you have called me to do. You are calling me to be your vessel and help with the healing, restoring and equipping of your daughters for the ministry. Oh Father, I think that you have the wrong person for the job. First of all, I am terrified to speak in front of people, I thinks its because of that gong show thing at school when I was young. Secondly, I am just now in the process of healing myself, I don't think that I would be of much help to anyone else and lastly Father, I am really a nobody. I am not a preacher. I am a housewife and mother and although these are great callings in themselves, I don't think that I am who you need. I can think of women right now who would be so much better at this calling. Father, I will do whatever you want me to do, but you are gonna have to open the doors and teach me to speak. I am willing Father, but I am afraid that willing is all that I am.

I realize that you have plans for me. Whatever those plans may be Father, I will do them for you.

You have just taken my breath away and touched the center of my heart. Whatever you want me to do, I will do. I am going to be amazed, though to see how your gonna restore the years that the locust stripped away. I love you my Savior, who has saved me yet again. You are my hero, my love and my future. Here I am Lord, make me of use for you. Thank you for this precious time with you and Father, may our tender contact never cease.

love,
your little girl

Dear daughter,

You are so welcome. I love to heal my children. I don't want my children to walk around with broken hearts and discouraged spirits. Oh yes, I have wonderful plans for you. Do you remember when you were a baby I told you that I had wonderful plans for you and I also told you that there would be times when you would forget that. Well it is time to remember my promises and to walk in them. I am going to use you and you will be a good servant and a daughter that will make any Father proud. Oh yes indeed, I know the plans that I have for you, so hold on…..as I begin to perfect those plans. The restoration now begins. The healing was step one and soon you will go through another step as I prepare you for my work. Love ya.

love,
your Pappa God

"THEN I WILL MAKE UP TO YOU FOR
THE YEARS THAT THE SWARMING LOCUST
HAS EATEN, THE CREEPING LOCUST, THE
STIPPING LOCUST, AND THE GNAWING
LOCUST, MY GREAT ARMY WHICH I SENT
AMONG YOU. AND YOU SHALL HAVE PLENTY
TO EAT AND BE SATISFIED, AND PRAISE THE
NAME OF THE LORD YOUR GOD, WHO HAS
DEALT WONDROUSLY WITH YOU; THEN MY
PEOPLE WILL NEVER BE PUT TO SHAME."
JOEL 2:25-26

LETTER #19

Dear Father,

It has been a year now since I received such massive forgiveness from you on that trip to Tulsa. A miracle has happened. You see, my husband was having a hard time with me going to church. He didn't understand my attraction and hunger for you. He was not raised as I was. He went to church when he was young, but I don't think that he ever had the kind of relationship that you and I have had. So whenever I would go off to church, he would be upset that I chose to go to church instead of stay home with him. Oh and I love him and want to be with him, but Father I can't stay away from the church. I am so in love with you and you are still healing old wounds and I love this precious time of healing and growing in you. Two weeks ago, my husband walked into the church with me and the children. A true miracle. He began to like Pastor Price and has become a member along with me. This is a precious gift to me. You are my life, you are my number one and to have my husband share that part of my life with me is so pleasing and important to me. He is on his way to falling in love with you just like I have. I want to thank you for that precious gift and for hearing the prayers of a hopeful wife and three tender sons.

Father, although I have grown tremendously and am even doing some teaching now, I still have such

a problem with my low self-esteem. It is so hard to
let go of the past. I still feel tarnished and scarred
up from the things done to me and the things that I
have done. I really need to shake this off. You keep
telling me to lift my head and walk with integrity and
boldness because I am your daughter. Oh, but I have
spent so many years being a misfit and a reject. I can't
help looking into the mirror sometimes and saying
"hey there's not much to look at is there."

Please forgive me for not appreciating me, your
creation. I am seeing that women seem to have a
tougher time letting go of the past and its effects
then men do. I can look at other women and see that
they too have been hurt or can't forgive themselves.
I guess that today is just a bad day for me. I was
recalling to my memory, that school that I went to
and the whole gong/talent show disaster. I remember
being picked on when I hadn't done anything to
anyone. I was simply teased because of who I was
and now you want me to celebrate who I am in you.
Its going to be difficult to appreciate the mirror again,
but Father, with your help I think that I can overcome
this unforgiveness for myself, after all look at all of
the seas that you have parted for me thus far. Give me
a word, now Father. A word of encouragement from
you is a surge of light and power to my soul. You are
my encourager among so much more and I love you.

love,
your little girl

Dear daughter,

My, my, my! You have such a hard time believing me. I tell you time and time again that I love you, that you are a new creation and the old you is dead and gone. Yet in your hard head you tend to choose the lies of the enemy over my truths. Don't forget that the mind is a battlefield, a major battlefield. The enemy will lie to you, tell you that you are and will always be trash. This is because I have great and wonderful plans for you and he's trying everything to hinder them. Don't listen to his lies, listen to me, I am your creator, your Father…I am your God and I say that you are clean, forgiven and a new creation. Now walk in this knowledge. Look in the mirror and see a daughter of the living God. I am God and I do not make trash. I love you, now get over the past and move on with me, just take your hands off of yesterday and place your hands on the hem of my robe and hold on to me. Look to me. Listen to me. Don't you know that the world considers my ways and my people foolish. You will always be an outcast from the world as long as you are in my will and living for me. Consider this an honor that you don't fit in. You are not supposed to fit in with the lost and judgmental world. You fit in with my family and baby there's no way that you could be a reject…because I would never reject you. You see your name is written in the palm of my hand and in the Lambs book of Life. You're somebody because you are mine.

love,
Your Pappa Father God

"FOR HE (JESUS) GREW UP BEFORE
HIM LIKE A TENDER SHOOT, AND LIKE A
ROOT OUT OF PARCHED GROUND; HE HAS
NO STATELY FORM OR MAJESTY THAT WE
SHOULD LOOK UPON HIM, NOR APPEARANCE
THAT WE SHOULD BE ATTRACTED TO HIM.
HE WAS DESPISED AND FORSAKEN OF MEN,
A MAN OF SORROWS, AND ACQUAINTED
WITH GRIEF; AND LIKE ONE FROM WHOM
MEN HIDE THEIR FACE, HE WAS DESPISED
AND WE DID NOT ESTEEM HIM. SURELY
OUR GRIEFS HE HIMSELF BORE; AND OUR
SORROWS HE CARRIED; YET WE OURSELVES
ESTEEMED HIM STRICKEN, SMITTEN OF
GOD, AND AFFLICTED. BUT HE WAS PIERCED
THROUGH FOR OUR TRANSGRESSIONS, HE
WAS CRUSHED FOR OUR INIQUITIES; THE
CHASTENING FOR OUR WELL-BEING FELL
UPON HIM, AND BY HIS SCOURGING WE ARE
HEALED. ALL OF US LIKE SHEEP HAVE GONE
ASTRAY, EACH OF US HAS TURNED TO HIS
OWN WAY; BUT THE LORD HAS CAUSED THE
INIQUITY OF US ALL…..TO FALL ON HIM."
ISAIAH 53:2-6

LETTER #20

Dear Father,

I have had a really bad day. I was scared for the life of one of my sons and then I experienced the power that comes from the name of Jesus. Let me explain…I am thirty two years old now Pappa and still each day brings its new lessons in the spiritual life and each day brings me closer to you. It is now in the evening and I am still getting over the shock of what happened to me today at the carwash.

I was at our local carwash that is about a half mile from my house. There is a convenience store right beside the carwash. My older two sons were at school and my husband at work. It was my two year old (my youngest) and me at the carwash. I was vacuuming out the van and I had noticed a very tall person standing against the outside wall of the convenience store looking at me. I could not tell if it was a man or a woman, but I could feel them watching me. I was bent down in the floor board of the front of my car vacuuming it out and my little son was in his car seat in the middle seat watching me and smiling at me. As I stood up there was a person standing right beside me. I jumped because I never heard them walk up to me. It was (after a moment of observing) a tall, rough looking woman, I'd say about my age, maybe a little older. I just looked at her and then she began to speak. She said "Lady, I need to use your van!" I just stared at her, not comprehending what she was saying, then I said "Excuse me?" Her voice became a little deeper and more stern as she said "I am going to take your van, I need it, I have to get across town and I need a car, so I am taking your van." My eyes immediately shifted to my little son in the car seat. Then what was taking place began to sink in and I told her "I can't let you have my van." It was her reply that brought fear into the picture as she said "Lady, I have a gun in this bag and I don't want to have to use it on you, but I need your van." I looked at the bag that she was holding in front of her. It was one of those white plastic grocery bags and from the shape of it, she was telling the truth. I froze, my mouth became very dry and my eyes again shifted to my baby boy in his car seat. "My son." I stammered. "I have to get my son out of the van." She did not reply but stepped even closer to me. I could feel her breath on my face. I was really scared, not for myself, but for my son, whom I was at that moment, prepared to take a bullet for. It was then that it happened. I will never be able to do justice in explaining the person that I became at that moment. I will never forget the forces that I felt taking place at that moment. Suddenly the fear was gone, like it was instantly removed from me and instead an awesome peace filled me and I felt a power like I have never felt before. I looked her dead in the eyes and said to her in a very calm but assertive voice, "Look, you cannot touch or hurt me or my child unless it is Gods time to take us home. If it is not His time to take us home, then there is absolutely nothing you can do to us because we are covered by and protected by the Blood of Jesus!" As I said this to her two things happened. The voice that I was speaking in became very loud and seemed to echo when I said "The Blood of Jesus!" also, when I spoke those words to her, that angry face transformed. Its like she melted right before my eyes. Tears began to fall down her face and she lowered her head and shook it a time or two and then said "I'm sorry ma'am, I am sorry," and she walked away shaking her head. I stood there feeling like I was standing on the top of a very large mountain and was untouchable. Then I jumped into the van, locked the doors, patted my son's chubby knee and looked out the window to see where she was going. She was gone. I could not see her anywhere. As I drove out of there I scanned the area for her, but to no avail. She was gone. Now she could have been a real person or she could have been a messenger of the enemy. I will never know, but there is something that I do know. I know that I have a lot of power at my disposal through Jesus. I also know that I will find myself in bad situations again and I will forget about this wonderful protection that you have given unto me through Jesus. As for today, I am just basking in how your rescued me once again. You have, for the most part, all of my life taken on all of my battles yourself, but today you let me fight a little. I think that I needed to know just how real and powerful you are. I saw a killer turn into a timid person in ten seconds. Those ten seconds that it took me to say "The Blood of Jesus!"

This incident today takes me back to a time when I was thirteen years old and I was living out in the country with my mom. It was dusk and we were walking down a deserted gravel road, just having an evening stroll. All of a sudden, from out of the woods came a pack of wild dogs. They were right at our heels and growling at us. I whispered "Mom, I am scared, those dogs are gonna get us." My mom said "Just don't look at them honey, keep walking and looking straight ahead." The dogs came closer to us and it was just a matter of seconds before they attacked us. It was then that my little, five foot tall mother turned around, pointed her finger at these dogs and in a very commanding voice said, "In the name of Jesus, get out of here!" Those dogs did exactly what she said. They lowered their eyes and heads, turned around and took off running back into the woods. My mom just turned back around, smiled and we continued our walk. Sitting here now, thinking about what happened back then and what happened today I have to say that right now I am admiring you in a big way. You are so cool God! And because I am your daughter I have at my disposal the very name that is above all names. The most powerful name to which one day every knee shall bow to…the name of Jesus. Thank you for reminding me of this today. Thank you for reminding me that I am not an orphan. That I am not a weakling. Thank you for reminding me today that I am a daughter of a great, great God. I love you

and once again I have to say that You are so cool…
God. In my book….you are the best.

love,

your little girl

Dear daughter,

This is sort of like Dorothy and those ruby red
shoes. She had the power all along and didn't know
it did she? The more that you believe in me and all
that I have given unto you through Jesus, the more
you will walk in this power. Remember what my
Word says came upon you when I filled you with my
Spirit…Power. If all of my children would believe
this, then we would see the miracles of old happening
today. Once again, though, you choose to believe the
lies of the enemy over my word. I have given you
children so many promises and I do not lie, yet the
enemy is made of destroying lies and yet my children
believe him more than Me. I love you children and
my patience never cease. However, it troubles me
that you pick and choose different parts of my word
to believe and not believe. You can understand why
your shadows don't heal the sick? Because YOU
don't believe in me that this can happen. I not only
believe, but know for a fact that this can happen. I
am up here in Heaven with my Holy hand extended
out to you, my children, and in my hand is power and
blessings but you won't take them from me. I have
already given you so much and I have so much more
to give you, but you won't take it. All you have to
do to receive from me is believe in the depth and the

height of my love for you. That's it. That simple…yet, that hard. Believe, my daughter. Have faith in me and I will become visible in you.

love,
your Pappa God

"BEHOLD, I HAVE GIVEN YOU AUTHORITY, TO TREAD UPON SERPENTS AND SCORPIONS, AND OVER ALL THE POWER OF THE ENEMY, AND NOTHING SHALL INJURE YOU. NEVERTHELESS DO NOT REJOICE IN THIS, THAT THE SPIRITS ARE SUBJECT TO YOU, BUT REJOICE THAT YOUR NAMES ARE RECORDED IN HEAVEN."

LUKE 10:19-20

"BUT YOU SHALL RECEIVE POWER WHEN THE HOLY SPIRIT HAS COME UPON YOU; AND YOU SHALL BE MY WITNESSES BOTH IN JERUSALEM, AND IN JUDEA AND SAMARIA, AND EVEN TO THE REMOTEST PART OF THE EARTH."

ACTS 1:8

LETTER #21

Dear Father,

This morning Father, I have experienced a liberty, a freedom, a release like I have never known. To be forgiven by you is my very oxygen, but I have experienced even more now, because I have finally forgiven and I now stand before you in the purest love for those who have once hurt me. I have forgiven those whom I have been angry at for twenty years.

A month ago I was asked by my pastor to be in a class that he calls "the Timothy class." This is a group of twelve people chosen by the pastor to meet with him once a week for few hours to learn how to be an effective leader and minister. My pastor shares with us his heart and experiences in the church and allows us to share our feelings and then we go into an in depth discussion of your word. My pastor had us read a book called "love, Acceptance and Forgiveness." As I read this book, I thought back to the church that kicked me out when I was fifteen. I expected to feel a bitterness towards these people as I thought about them and re-lived every moment in my memory of that day twenty years ago. Father, it was not bitterness that I felt towards them .You see, I had been told by many people and seen a little of it myself, that this church fell apart after they had kicked me out. I heard about painful things happening to the people that dealt with me. I had seen some of them after that day

and they were not the same people. They had lost
all of the fruits of the Spirit. They were angry, bitter
and had major family problems. As I thought about
them and their misfortunes I began to weep. Father,
I was weeping for them. I know that you say that
vengeance is yours and I respect that, but you know
I began to wonder if what happened to those people
had anything to do with what they did to me. I know
that you heard me at that moment when I came to you
on my knees and my heart released this anger that I
had for these people and embraced a compassion for
them in angers place. Do you remember what I said
to you at that moment? I said "Father, if these people
are hurting still, twenty years later and if its because
of me, I beg of you…let them go. Lets let this whole
thing go. Father, bless them, Make up for them the
years the locusts had stripped away, please, they are
not just people, they are my brothers and sisters in
Christ and I forgive them, Father. Now I ask with all
of my heart that you forgive them and that you heal
them and bless them and give back to them the joy of
your salvation."

Oh Father, as I said these words to you, I felt a love
in my heart for them and I am totally surrounded by
peace and sweet freedom. I can still see the faces
of these men and women and I ask you to fill their
faces with smiles and peace. Put them back into
the ministry if they are out. Maybe, they have been
doing well for many years, in that case, bless them
even more. As I read this book on love, forgiving
and accepting, I have realized that without your love

alive in all of us, we are not capable of forgiving or accepting anyone. To be able to sit here and feel this tremendous love for these people is a personal victory for me and a major step forward. Most of all though, Father, I know that I am deeply in love with you, because whatever I do unto them, I have done to you. To love them, purely….is to love you deeply. To forgive them completely….is to accept your forgiveness in total faith and whole-heartedly. I even accept what they did as something that they did out of fear and I understand that today. I believe that they truly thought since I had committed fornication that I had evil spirits about me and they were afraid for their own children. Being a mother myself now, I can understand their misplaced fears. I have been around some of the sweetest, Christians, who truly love you and seen them mess up or say things that hurt another. I know that the enemy uses every opportunity he can to stop us from loving and serving you. At that moment, twenty years ago, they were just used by the enemy to stop me in my spiritual tracks, but this does not mean that they were bad people. In fact they are good people and I have learned so much, even in my darkest disasters. I wanted you to know Father that the proof is indeed in the pudding and that I do dearly and tenderly love you, because I love them. I also wanted you to know the biggest lesson of all that I have learned from this and that I pray you will give me the opportunity to pass on to the body. I have learned that no matter who walks through the doors of the church, no matter what they

look like or act like...I will love them and accept
them for who they are. I have learned that one wrong
word to a person can destroy their lives. I know how
much you loved me through all of this mess and I am
to love people with your love. The church is for the
messed up, broken hearted sinners. The worse they
are...the more they need love, comfort, acceptance
and to see you in my face and actions. I love you my
precious Father. You have shown me so much. You
have restored to me the years that the locusts stripped
away. I would have never made it without your love.
Your mercy has impressed my heart so much that I
clearly see the power of it. With this love and mercy
I now set out to love the unlovable and to reach the
unreachable and to touch the untouchable. Why?
Because I could never ever forget how you reached
me when I was unreachable. I am so changed today
because you reached me when I was unreachable. I
am so changed today because you touched me when I
was untouchable and Father, I am so in love with you
because you loved me when I was unlovable. Thank
you Jesus...for being the first and greatest influence
of love in my life. Thank you. I smile now, because
I love and I know that right now on your Holy Face
there is a smile....because I love. Bless them Father
and lets move ahead.

love,
your little girl

Dear daughter,

I know all that you have been through and every incident that happened to you has made you who you are today. I keep my promises and I have promised to restore to you those years and to complete my plans for you. Look at you now. Teaching, loving, giving and walking hand in hand with me. Just look at you....Daddy's little girl. I am proud of you. You have learned priceless treasures of wisdom that I will indeed give you the opportunity to pass on to others. Just as I have forgiven you many times, so do I forgive all of my children when they ask me to, including those in your past. No, I do not have a jar of forgiveness with each persons name on it that runs out. My forgiveness is an eternal fountain that never dries up. I love you. I am glad that you went into that Timothy class, just as I had planned for you to. I work all things out for the good for those who love me…don't I? You are living proof of that aren't you? Your home, your children, your husband, your ministry…your heart. Now pass it on honey……Now pass it on…..this love that…..you are walking in…. pass it on. I also know that right now you are standing in a victory, but your race is not over yet. More trials will come your way, remember the depth of my love for you and you will have a time of victory following each trial.

love,
Your Pappa God

"AND WHENEVER YOU STAND PRAYING,
FORGIVE, IF YOU HAVE ANYTHING AGAINST
ANYONE; SO THAT YOUR FATHER WHO
IS IN HEAVEN MAY FORGIVE YOU YOUR
TRANSGRESSIONS. BUT IF YOU DO NOT
FORGIVE, NEITHER WILL YOUR FATHER
WHO IS IN HEAVEN FORGIVE YOUR
TRANSGRESSIONS."
MARK 11:25-26

"IF I SPEAK WITH THE TONGUES OF
MEN AND OF ANGELS, BUT DO NOT HAVE
LOVE, I HAVE BECOME A NOISY GONG OR A
CLANGING CYMBAL. AND IF I HAVE THE GIFT
OF PROPHECY, AND KNOW ALL MYSTERIES
AND ALL KNOWLEDGE; AND IF I HAVE ALL
FAITH, SO AS TO REMOVE MOUNTAINS, BUT
DO NOT HAVE LOVE, I AM NOTHING. AND
IF I GIVE ALL MY POSSESSIONS TO FEED
THE POOR, AND IF I DELIVER MY BODY TO
BE BURNED, BUT DO NOT HAVE LOVE, IT
PROFITS ME NOTHING. LOVE IS PATIENT,
LOVE IS KIND, AND IS NOT JEALOUS; LOVE
DOES NOT BRAG AND IS NOT ARROGANT,
DOES NOT ACT UNBECOMINGLY; IT DOES
NOT SEEK ITS OWN, IS NOT PROVOKED,
DOES NOT TAKE INTO ACCOUNT A
WRONG SUFFERED, DOES NOT REJOICE IN
UNRIGHTEOUSNESS, BUT REJOICES WITH
THE TRUTH; BEARS ALL THINGS, BELIEVES

ALL THINGS, HOPES ALL THINGS, ENDURES
ALL THINGS. LOVE NEVER FAILS."
I CORINTIANS 13:1-8

LETTER #22 THE FINAL LETTER

Dear Father,

I titled this letter "the final letter," of course that isn't all together true. I will continue to write to you every day of my life. I want to pass on this book to everyone in search of you and your love so I had to end it somewhere for now. I never know what you're gonna do, so there may be a second book of letters later. For now though I think that I have written enough to get out vital messages to the readers. Oh Father, I ask now that you would bless this book with YOUR blessings so that many others can look back on their journeys and see the bigger picture. I know that there were hundreds of times in my life when I said "why me, why is this happening to me?" Now, I know exactly why me! I have come to the conclusion that this book serves three purposes. The first and most important…to give you glory! The second purpose, to minister to my brothers and sisters your unconditional love. Now the third purpose I did not realize until about halfway through this book, then I saw what you were doing. I wrote this for me also. As I went through the past, trudging, crawling and sometimes flying I began to see how you worked each event out for my good. There were so many things that I went through in my life that I did not write about in this book that hurt really bad or messes that I got myself into that were pretty messy. So, I have taken a visit to see my yesterday while writing this book. I have cried, prayed, laughed, praised you, questioned you, regretted, hoped and loved you all through this book. You have even brought to my attention some old wounds that were still open and you closed them with loving finality. I sit here now and smile up at you…my hero and the love of my lifetime. I know now after the menagerie of beasts I have fought in the past that I can go up to many hurting people, put my arms around them and be able to in all honesty say, "I understand, I know how you feel." If I had been spared one of the nightmares of my past, it would be one less person that I could minister to. I thank you for my life Father. I thank you for each trial and temptation. I thank you for each wound and tear, for without them I would never know how to forgive, move on, love unconditionally and reach others. You have taken a life that could have destroyed me and instead turned it around for my better and for your glory.

Now Father, I conclude this book by asking that You bless each reader with healing as your have healed me. I ask Father, that you reveal to each reader the steadfastness of your love, the power of your mercy and the endlessness of your forgiveness towards them. Oh Father, that we, your children would totally grasp the depth of your love for us. Oh, sweet Pappa God, I pray that we, your children would hold fast to your promises for our futures. I love you.

You have given me life and life abundantly. I am truly successful, because I am your daughter and together we have fought the lions, survived the stormy seas, stayed a float in our arks, torn down the high places, walked away from the wells anew, rebuilt the temple walls, torn other walls down with a shout and fought off our Goliaths. I was never alone in any of these battles….was I? You, whom I call faithful and true. You never left me and you will never leave me. For this reason, I give you this book to do with it what you will in the wonderful name of Jesus. AMEN! And with much love….your little girl.

"BUT HE KNOWS THE WAY I TAKE; WHEN HE HAS TRIED ME, I SHALL COME FORTH AS GOLD."
                          JOB 23:10

ABOUT THE AUTHOR

Melissa Flemming lives in Houston with her husband and three sons. She is a graduate of the school of hard knocks. She graduated with honors in endurance and experience. She attends Houston Northwest Foursquare Church (life Church) in Houston and wishes to extend a special thank you to Pastors J.P. and Hollie Price for their love and acceptance that assisted her back to the cross. Melissa teaches in the children's ministry and ladies ministry. She has been a member at her church for six years and attended many teaching workshops and discipleship classes. She was born in 1965 in Jos, Nigeria, where her parents were missionaries with Sudan Missions. Melissa is also the author of "AND I THOUGHT I WAS ALONE" and "ABBA HERO".

"Letters to my Father" is the 3rd book that Melissa has written. Melissa writes in her spare time while raising 3 sons. Since the day of her birth, Melissa has survived many tough situations, and close calls. Because her life has been a colorful one, she has chosen to use it as the tool for writing "Letters to my Father". Melissa is the ladies group leader at the Houston N.W. Foursquare Church and loves to teach the women there as well as take them on retreats in her home state of Texas. Her greatest hope for her books is that they leave the reader full where once they were empty, hopeful where once they were sad, and most of all, that they leave the reader smiling, where once they were not.

www.ingramcontent.com/pod-product-compliance
Lightning Source LLC
Chambersburg PA
CBHW030351290526
45785CB00004B/1701